Garland, Maine and the Old Maple Tree: Windows from My Soul

Judy Bagley Welch

Garland, Maine and the Old Maple Tree:
Windows from My Soul

Copyright © 2011 by Judy Bagley Welch

All rights reserved under the International and Pan-American copyright conventions. No part of this book may be reproduced, stored in a retrieval system, or transmitted in any form, electronic, mechanical, or by other means, without written permission of the author.

Library of Congress
Cataloging in Publication Data

ISBN 978-0-94598-076-6

North Country Press
Unity, Maine

Dedicated to my son Heath for bringing love and light to my life, for choosing me as your mom

Acknowledgements

A very special thank you to Eber & Wein Publishing for all their help and support during the first printing of this book. I wish to thank all my family and lifelong friends for all their encouragement and experiences while on this journey, though not aware I could write a serious book. I have been holding this card in my hand for many years, though unaware--I thought, no better time than now to play it. I hope this book makes you smile and I hope you're enjoying your favorite beverage while reading it. May it also bring a form of healing to you, as it has done for me while writing it.

From my heart to yours,
Judy Bagley Welch

Contents

When You Walk with Your Hand in the Lord's	1
Listen, My Journey Starts	2
Searching	4
Still Searching	4
Leaving	5
Seeing	5
The Great Maple Tree	6
Changing	7
Us Seven Children	8
Peepers	8
Where Will Our Journeys Take Us?	9
My Two Granddaughters and I—Nana	10
Five Boys, Two Girls	11
Clouds	12
Me—Lying in Bed	13
Ice Skating—Our Father Teaching His Two Oldest Grandsons to Ice Skate	14
Prebbles Brook	16
Mission Accomplished—Our Father Teaching Us to Fly a Kite	17
My Stone	18
Letting Go a Little	19
Growing	20
Our Parents	21
Springtime—Our Father's Flowers	21
Larry	22
Hunting Season	23
My Robin—Dianne	24
My Sister—Mary	25
Our Father	26
Windows from My Soul—Our Mom Making Pies	27
Rings in My Old Tree	28

My Roots	29
Senses and Sounds	30
The Old Register	31
Planting a Garden	32
Dollies and Truck Dollies	32
January	33
My Eyes—Life	33
Broken Fences—Childhood Memories	34
Cellar Stairs—Our Home	35
The Cane—My Brother Made for Me	36
Apple Blossom Petals— Seven Children Before School	37
Stain Colored Glass	38
Piggy Back Rides—My Sister and I	39
Shutters—My Family	40
Driveway—A Dear Old Friend	41
A Dream—a Vision	42
Fishing Tackle Basket—My Five Brothers	43
Attic of an Old Farmhouse	44
Neighbor—Stranger	45
Riding on Angel Wings—A Dream	46
Oliver Hill	47
Plowing of a Field	48
The Gift—My Writing, a Vision	49
The Old Plow Truck and I	50
My Tiny Little Shealyn Rose—Heart Surgery	52
Tea Time	53
Mommy's Piggytails, Braids, Ponytails and Ribbons	54
Daddy's Home—My Two Granddaughters and Daddy's Log Truck	55
Maine Truckers—To My Son	56
Pipe Organs	59
The Old Pot	60
I'll Wait	61
Past and Future	62

Family, Friend, Feast	63
Today I Received My Class One—My Son Teaching Me on the Golden Road with My Permit	64
The Watering Hole Gathering	65
Whispers, Giggles, Grins	66
Swing	67
Boards, Knot, One Hole	68
Thoughts, Dreams, Visions	69
Pig Skin	71
Five Linemen	72
My Son—Three Times You Came	73
Yesterday	75
One Name Upon an Envelope	77
Snow Angels and Snow Bunnies	78
Old Rags, Old Rug, New Yarn, New Flag	80
"Nana, What Does God Look Like?"	82
Christmas Tea	83
Apron Strings and Wings—To My Loving Son Heath Bagley	84
Team of Great White Horses—In Memory of My Youngest Brother Larry	86
Last Night, Beside My Bed, I Knelt	87
The Great Tree Stand	88
Silently, I Wait	90

Garland, Maine and the Old Maple Tree: Windows from My Soul

When You Walk with Your Hand in the Lord's
Written by my mother, Alice Christina Fickett Bagley

In all walks of life there are sorrows,
In all walks of life there are joys.
But to me, the most peaceful walk
Is when you walk with your hand in the Lord's.

No matter how deep your sorrows may seem,
No matter how great are your joys,
You too can have a peaceful walk
If you walk with your hand in the Lord's.

So when you feel tired and weary
And your sorrows seem more than your joys,
Just think of what Jesus has told you,
And walk with your hand in the Lord's.

Judy Bagley Welch

Listen, My Journey Starts

Wolves, coyotes, pipes, flutes
I'm on a journey to find myself
deep within my soul
I've searched a long time, just like
anyone else.
We don't really know how or why
I don't like the word why—
It leaves the door too open
to many questions to answer
The drums and flutes
will play again, as they dance
in my mind or imagination, wondering
where I will go next—
I might write of two
beautiful young sprites, which I
Love dearly—
so innocent and carefree
like the colors of a double rainbow
or two butterflies in flight—
that's what my eyes and imagination see.
Longing to spread their wings
on a long and inspirational journey,
not knowing where those wings
will take them in flight
The thunder comes as also
the howls of a lonesome coyote
What is it he is howling for?
"I do not know" a home from
where he has traveled far—and lost his way—

Garland, Maine and the Old Maple Tree: Windows from My Soul

I shiver at the sounds of
the howls, as chills go all over
my body—
"Silence" for I know
I'm okay!

It's very spiritual to me and
lets me know and assures me
I'm close to my creator!

As the thunder roars, and the
lightning crackles, lighting up
the heavens, for thousands
of years before—but we are
too afraid to actually look up to.

Judy Bagley Welch

Searching

Water running, birds singing
harmonic tunes in sequence
with Mother Earth, everything
seems right!

Listen—you shall hear
the children playing, oh so
innocent, carefree, from running
through a mud puddle after
a thunder storm,
listening to a "whooperwill"
at the edge of darkness,
Life stands still—as good nights
and prayers are being said.

Still Searching

Flutes, playing as I long for home,
I've been to and long to go back to—
forgetting about it, though still in
my mind, for I not know
or have not forgotten
I still yearn to go there
it is where we are most
comfortable with, but have
chose not to remember now—
But is in us all—
forever to remember!

Garland, Maine and the Old Maple Tree: Windows from My Soul

Leaving

Pups young at heart
playful, carefree
learning from their parents
hard times, survival, caring
for, nurturing, protecting their
siblings, until its time
to leave—taking all they
have gathered and been
taught, in hopes to make
a better way of life
for their families!

Seeing

Flutes, horns—calling from a distance—
A beautiful sunset, to a red sunrise!
Dew on a rose petal early in the
morning, to ripples on a silent
lake in the evening
a loon dipping in for a peek
an eagle overhead waiting—
A dragonfly hovering in flight—
waiting for just the right moment
a frog setting on a lily-pad in silence
Droplets of rain dance on
the lake, spiraling circles of who knows where
and when they will stop
The thunder roars—lightning lights
the heavens and the full rain begins to fall,
I hear the loons and coyotes in the distance
Knowing all is okay—tomorrow, a new day!

Judy Bagley Welch

The Great Maple Tree

Am I afraid? For I do not
Know if I am!
Come to me
I'm waiting
I will wait patiently in wonder
Not knowing what I wait for
I sense you are close
I'm not afraid
I hear the rustling, I tremble
with anticipation—
I'm not afraid
I hear the sound and still,
I'm not afraid—
Come to me
I'll wait in silence!
I'm listening and hear you
I do not know—
Talk to me!
I hear you and I see you,
smell, taste, touch you—
You are the breath in me!
The Great Maple Tree!

Garland, Maine and the Old Maple Tree: Windows from My Soul

Changing

I smile, thinking about what I
may write next—
Thinking—nothing comes to me—
mind is so full of many memories
my pen gets caught up in my
thoughts—I hesitate!

Recipes—parents
That's what we are like—
A recipe—
We have been taught to believe
in certain ways, live certain ways
I'm finding out I know now
it's okay to change the recipe in
Your life—
that's why we are all here,
to be able to make your own
chocolate cake, bake your own beans
I could never make my mom's beans,
So I have my own recipe.
Thinking—I should just
keep trying, wasn't working
took me many years to understand
it's okay to be yourself—life goes on
In other words it's okay to let go
try your own recipe,
sometimes by doing things your own way—
you may feel you have given up
betraying—Not true! It's okay to let go,
I know this now, life is like the
beans or cake, take only what you need
and leave the rest.

Judy Bagley Welch

Us Seven Children

I look out across the glistening
snow, as an old leaf scurries
on its way to who knows where
Feeling the sun warm my face.
In my mind, I'm that leaf—
Like a little child
sliding on a new sled.
Wind on my face,
Chill on my nose—thinking of nothing
I scurry back, unlike the
leaf still blowing
I slide again!
It's so wonderful to be that
child and become that little
leaf—If just for one moment.
Smile! For I know it is in you
also.

Peepers

Peepers, just waiting for that evening
when their voices will be heard again
the icy waters are melting
from the spring sunshine,
Knowing new life will be coming soon—
As they know and they too
Shall become something new also.

Where Will Our Journeys Take Us?

Where will our journeys take us?
Through the voices of the birds?
I hear their singing—a duck
quacking overhead, only to be
going on its journey
somewhere in flight—
not knowing where,
just going where the wind will take it,
stopping here and there—
gathering new ideas,
only to fly back—where it has come from—
The beauty of an eagle in flight,
just waiting, soaring, hovering in the air—
so peaceful, graceful, beautiful—
for I am that eagle
as we all are!

Judy Bagley Welch

My Two Granddaughters and I—Nana

A trout swimming through the waves
of life, never knowing when the
next raindrop or fly will be
just the right one—
He swims in awe and
anticipation, as we all do in our lives,
waiting for the right moment to be
given to us—
We take it!
Sometimes scary, sometimes exciting,
but we take it,
only to learn something
new about ourselves.

I hear the frogs, something new
on the horizon
take it—Listen? It's unfolding
like the new petals of a newborn
Water-lily, or petals of a newborn
Rose in bloom!
Go in them—feel, touch,
smell, taste, see them
For they are who we are
in all their beauty.

Garland, Maine and the Old Maple Tree: Windows from My Soul

Five Boys, Two Girls

Spring rains,
puddles, mud, running.
Laughing, smelling the
fresh new air after the
long winter—
the warmth of the water
on our feet
feel the mud between
our toes
splashing, nothing to
worry about!
Sunshine and warm
summer rain—go there,
if only in your imagination
Go there!
Experience it!
It's in us all!

Judy Bagley Welch

Clouds

Clouds, pouring in—some soft
and subtle, some dark and gray
I watch! Waiting—what
will come next? Will rain
overpower the sunshine?
Birds singing
Thunder roars in the distance
They both work together—
I see beauty
I see the rainbow,
another day to play in the
puddles of life
So I take it, for it
belongs to not only me,
but to us all—
Take it.

Garland, Maine and the Old Maple Tree: Windows from My Soul

Me—Lying in Bed

I hear the coyotes in the distance
over the hill, as I lie nestled in my bed—
I listen to what they are trying to teach me,
for they have a story in them
also to share, just as we all do.
Look deep within your soul,
it is there, you will find it,
just like the howls of the coyote, longing for home.
Voices from them, crying for a home so far away
but still within its reach—
echoes through my mind
like paths through my
childhood, or like the air
you blow through a flute
or a horn, is like the
blood that runs through our
veins at birth and we live.

Judy Bagley Welch

Ice Skating—Our Father Teaching His Two Oldest Grandsons to Ice Skate

Swirling, like a beautiful swan
in the water, my imagination
takes me there!
I am that swan, on a
frozen piece of water that
has been splashed across a field,
only to see reflection in it
from the wind on a winter night,
covered with cow-patties,
with glimes of soft snow
that had fallen the night before—
Smiling through the insecurities you may
have in your life
Go there! For you too
shall perhaps see a childhood
memory that has been lodged in you,
take that moment,
treasure it—for it belongs to you.
Again, a little field mouse,
scurrying along its way
reaches the snow-covered cow-patties—
then realizing it's gone—
only to be solid, he takes his time,
cautiously sliding across the ice,
for he is also like the swan,
after he reaches the snow again!

Garland, Maine and the Old Maple Tree: Windows from My Soul

Close to his home,
familiar to him—he then becomes
more so like the swan again.
I smile watching
with anticipation—a giggle
out loud—He is back up
and on his merry way,
he scampers into a hole that
has become his very own home,
he treasures it, until again
he scampers through a field or a stream
for He is safe there—

Judy Bagley Welch

Prebbles Brook

A babbling brook, the singing of
beautiful birds in the distance
for—I swim like a trout
through life in this brook
crows cawing overhead
Life stands still
If just for a moment, I am
that trout, many wonderful
and unexplainable things to
look at as I splash through
the water of my life
in this brook.
Go there, it's yours also!
Swim like that little trout,
so peaceful, carefree, not
knowing where it will lead him—
Who knows? Just go there.
The stream or brook of
life has many things to offer,
Take them! For they are
ours or yours—
Bends in a brook, curves upstream,
like the life of a great salmon,
we will also spawn in life,
If we just choose to go
where we dare not!

Mission Accomplished—Our Father Teaching Us How to Fly a Kite

Wind whistling through the trees
at the end of a long cold
winter's night
Everything being reborn,
little flowers peeping out
a new birth—to
see what's new
soft spring air with
a bite of winter still in it,
birds coming home from a long journey—
like a kite with
the longest tail, flying high like the birds above
what a beautiful sight and sound
Wind blowing through its feathers, it swallows
your kite high up towards the heavens.
Down, the wind shifts!
Down it comes, like a baby
bird on his first flight with
his new wings—safe—at last
only to try again
never giving up—for he
knows it's his mission to
accomplish—"He" does!

My Stone

A stone
Finding just the right one
Like an owl—who?!
shall we become?
Strong, like the great bear,
wise as the owl, graceful
as the deer, or sly as the fox
I've wondered many years
I have wondered
the softness of a daisy petal,
thorns on a beautiful rose,
or like a bunny rabbit
gone from his mommy for the first time,
Exploring, I stop!
Listen, look, feel—
have I found my stone?
Is it strong enough to
withstand the obstacles
that enter into my hands
that comes my way?
Or do I find another?
For I do not know.
I'm willing to try again—
for I know it's meant to be—
Find your stone, make it yours, and only yours—
hold it close, cherish it, learn from it—
become that stone, become that owl, or that bear!
Carry your stone everywhere!

Letting Go a Little

Birds in flight—looking for just the right branch
to land on, a baby fawn, running through a field of daisies,
jumping, living life to the fullest—
so carefree, unaware—Mom is watching—
with her eyes so intense upon her new baby,
never too far—still insight—
not afraid to let it go
a little further away at a time,
But still within its reach
Until
She knows the day is
closing in, and she too,
will start again—
Another birth, and life!

Judy Bagley Welch

Growing

Darkness overcomes the light of day
all is still, in our imagination—
"we sleep"—wondering
what tomorrow may bring
Dreams of butterflies
and robins—
tasting their first
flower or their first droplet
of the new morning dew
go there in your mind
taste the flower of spring
and the dew upon your lips!
Reawaken to a whole new day—
Take it as if your first.
Feel the rays of the sunshine warm your soul
Go into it, it's yours!
Mold it like a piece of clay—
It's a precious gift,
playful as a puppy or a new kitten
with a piece of string,
twirling around in the rays of life,
like a beautiful may pole dance!
Colors of the rainbow, after a hard,
piercing thunderstorm,
All is still!
Smell the freshness of the wind
after a spring rain, see the clouds
Go there! It's beautiful.
Dance the dance, sing the songs of the birds in flight.
Bees buzzing, hunting for the perfect lilac or sweetpea—
This is the dance of life! It's free—take it!
For tomorrow is a new day!

Our Parents

Morning doves, soaring in flight
Mountains in the distance
they stay together—
flying side by side
Though sometimes seemed impossible,
soaring through obstacles,
Ups and downs, across and over,
between—they sing in perfect harmony
with nature and themselves—
for they are mates for eternity!

Springtime—Our Father's Flowers

Crows cawing in the distance,
a robin finding the right worm, trees so still and tall,
snow hangs upon their limbs—
Waiting in anticipation—for the first drop of an icicle
From a maple tree, tasting it on my tongue,
oh so sweet!
Like the smell of a freshly picked
bouquet of sweet peas, or a beautiful dahlia
that has just budded,
the winter subsides—spring has come back
with Raging Glory!
A new beginning had been born!

Judy Bagley Welch

Larry

A little bee buzzing through life,
hunting for just the right flower
to stop at—
smelling, admiring, hurrying, also
like little ants, knowing not
where their journeys are going
to take them
Obstructions, come out of nowhere,
muddy waters, the heavy rains—
Then thunder and lightning.
In the distance, a beautiful rainbow,
and rays of sunshine
perfect as the day we were born,
and we know, we will be going
as quickly as they came,
knowing that the muddy waters
will subside and take us to
where we know so well—
and are most comfortable!
Home.

Hunting Season

An acorn falling to the ground
A little squirrel, waiting silently
to gather it—
A beautiful buck in
freshly new velvet
Waiting—still as the wind,
ears listening like a hawk—
not knowing!
Just waiting
Then with eyes so intense
Boom! Thunder!
Unsteady as to what has happened, for he gave,
you took, survival.
Life goes on—
A new life begins—for it's
a circle and is not lost.

Judy Bagley Welch

My Robin—Dianne

A robin flying home in the spring
from where I do not know
Hopping along, gathering twigs,
branches, only to start a
new beginning
Bringing tools to help someone
along the way
Unaware of the stream
of life that it has brought,
merrily it keeps going
expecting nothing in return—
It takes a worm to
fill its belly, then goes along
on its merry way, gathering life's
tools again—placing them just
where they are supposed to be—
Then bringing life to it—
Blue the color of the sky!
Warmth from her feathers, chirping,
Singing a sweet melody, as she
brings them to life!

Garland, Maine and the Old Maple Tree: Windows from My Soul

My Sister—Mary

Oh—little groundhog—woodchuck
Do not be afraid
things are so familiar to you—
Yet you hesitate, waiting,
wanting to—
you peek out again, feeling
the warmth of sunshine on
your little nose—
You hesitate, still unsure!
Then you burst out
playing, scampering with your
family, for you knew when
the time was right, still unsure
of everything, you're cautious,
smelling everything that is new again—
Exploring new ground, new lessons
to be learned, as well as taught—
You take them, you teach them,
share them—
You know who you are.
Still not quite sure what is ahead,
you go on, over little hills, rocks, twigs,
never giving up—you go on.
Be that rainbow that has been you
for so many years—
Unfold it, shape it, for it's your rainbow
to do as you feel—
Come see your rainbow!
It's waiting
just for you!

Judy Bagley Welch

Our Father

The snarls of the mighty bear
as piercing as a screech owl!
You come out only to find
it's not quite time
you wait—longing for, you're
not sure
again, I see caring for
your young, in a way you have
been taught
But many lessons you
need to learn still,
playful at times, excited, somber
But you teach in ways that
someday—you also will understand the lesson,
you have so tried to pass on—

Windows from My Soul—Our Mom Making Pies

I dare peep through
for I am older now
a little higher up my tree
I look, I see,
beautiful hands, splashed
with the touch of flour, ready
and so steady for the crust
of life, to be laid down so gently
I watch in awe
as the berries are poured
spilling into the crust of
life that has just been made
so sweet! The taste, the smell,
as if a new day
just arrived
For I am there!
If only in my tree of life
I see through the
windows of my soul
And—I remember—

Judy Bagley Welch

Rings in My Old Tree

I turn around, like the rings
in my old tree, that shows its age—
from broken branches to new buds
that has just sprouted
I see children scampering with their
new sleds on fresh new snow
that had fallen the night before
pulling, running, laughing, no worries!
To be the old tree—to see through
its rings of life—
Oh what a gift—
Look deep within—
You too may also
see the children through
its rings
A complete circle
No beginning, no end.

Garland, Maine and the Old Maple Tree: Windows from My Soul

My Roots

Roots, deep within the earth's dirt
that holds my tree so strong—
waiting, unknown, what's next?
A new bud, a new branch, to learn from,
Are my roots strong enough to hold them?
For I am still growing—
Many seasons pass—
Some branches gone with the seasons—
only to find a new one—
Again my roots run deep
another ring,
another beginning,
another branch of my life has been born—
I turn again, smelling the sap that
runs through my branches.
I see an old dirt road, traveled
by so many, played on by many—
Again, another ring.
Who walked this old road before?
I do not know—before my roots
were planted here, I wonder.
Many leaves have fallen, only to return again,
more vibrant, more beautiful for the next one
to wonder about that may walk this old road.
My leaves are gone, but not forgotten,
for I will return with sweet sap for you to take from me
and in return, I shall give you beautiful colors to hold, if not in your
hands and mind, at least in your heart. Taste my sap, touch my rough
bark—for I am here for you—my roots live on!

Judy Bagley Welch

Senses and Sounds

Crickets, grasshoppers
Scurrying on their way
I see through my branches at
the amazement, the wind blows
a smile through the limbs of my life—
I stand tall and watch life in motion,
as it goes around me,
through me, up me, I'm amazed!
Evening approaches, I hear through my leaves—
the different sounds, for the day soon will be gone,
I hear the sweet song of a "whooperwill" music to my ears
as I know so well—a new day
will be born tomorrow—
Again I will learn as I peek through the windows of life,
We all know so well.

Garland, Maine and the Old Maple Tree: Windows from My Soul

The Old Register

Peeking through the panes of an old homestead
Yearning to catch a glimpse of the past—
Where it began—in awe,
I wonder! For what I might see,
a roaring fire, that warms the souls that live there—
Snow dripping from a mitten
placed on a register above,
bouncing with sound, as it hits just right!
Bringing a smile on the children's faces,
It bubbles like giggling in anticipation
from the child within us—
as it reaches its final destination.

Judy Bagley Welch

Planting a Garden

Sweet harvest, strong hands,
covered with the earth's dirt
that's beneath my roots—
smelling the dirt that has
been taken, only to be returned,
covering a tiny seed that has just been sown,
waiting, watching in the distance
for its little head to burst through the earth!
Showing those strong hands
how "gentle" they sometimes were!

Dollies and Truck Dollies

So precious, strong, teaching
not knowing what
From holding up iron beneath a trailer,
lighting up the eyes of
a child on a beautiful morning
many lessons inside
an elderly woman's face—
teaching them to so many!

January

January, a new birth, a new ring
in the air—as within my roots,
my sun/"son" is born!
Life again!
I see a different ring
the sweet bitterness of leaving
For I lost a branch (my mother)
only to give birth to a new one
(my son)
The sweetness of the sap and
the sting of the break
for it's the circle!
Another ring of life.
I continue growing
Stronger!

My Eyes—Life

Mosquitoes, black flies
swarming in flight, after
a new rain,
new cut grass,
hay being cut, swirling, buzzing,
stinging,
Still—beauty
For they too—also have
a journey!

Judy Bagley Welch

Broken Fences—Childhood Memories

Broken fences, walking gently
through—
They will follow
down the countryside to
a field that appears so much greener
One by one
Still young—pastured out
for the first time
running, jumping
chasing one another
stopping to graze
tasting to new grasses
beyond the
Broken Fences!

Cellar Stairs—Our Home

Another windowpane
I glance! Do I dare
peek through?
I must
Like the cellar stairs!
Do I go down?
I must—
not for long!
One step at a time
creaking, moving beneath my feet
I continue!
The last one—
Now on the dirt floor—
smelling the old earth
that has been there for years
Looking around—
I gather,
Hurrying, almost running
to get to the top of the
old cellar stairs—
shutting the door quickly
Until it's time—
to gather again!

Judy Bagley Welch

The Cane—My Brother Made for Me

You found me beneath a brush pile—
Beauty not aware
You took me home
worked with me—
Molding me through your eyes!
For you knew
whom to give
this precious piece of wood.

Apple Blossom Petals—Seven Children Before School

Apple blossom petals
Touched by hands as soft
and smooth as apple blossom petals,
touch our faces and smell
sweet as well
Wake up! Wake up!
It's morn,
frost on a nail head
a new day being born,
the hands that touched the
many cheeks, have made
the oats and biscuits feel soft
as apple blossoms
Smell the blossoms "Oh so sweet!"
Come sit, my little faces!
Come sit!
For we shall all eat!

Judy Bagley Welch

Stain Colored Glass

Stain colored glass
Oh what beauty you withhold
stories to be told—
I see through the beauty of
the many lives you have touched
the flaws—yellow with
pain, I go there still
peeking through another pane
to find the peace within.
Smiles mostly,
A kind word,
A story to be told,
I look around and I see
through the stain-colored glass,
What used to be!
And I smile!

Garland, Maine and the Old Maple Tree: Windows from My Soul

Piggy Back Rides—My Sister and I

Smaller than you
I carry you—for you
shall carry me back
the hill I carried
You down
I giggle
wondering, waiting, seems
far away—For I am
Smaller, but I still carried you—
for someday, I too
shall get my piggy back
ride from you up that hill—
to be always by my side!

Judy Bagley Welch

Shutters—My Family

Shutters
like the lens of a camera
opening when you choose
Look through,
watch, scan them, through
your eyes, for they are your
pictures, only to share if you choose.
Sad, scary, happy,
live them again from time to time—
For they are a form of healing—
like the shutters in your mind!

Driveway—A Dear Old Friend

A snow-covered path
just been touched again
by fresh fallen snow
A noise I hear!
A familiar face
I see!
A friend from long ago
Lending a hand to a friend in need
not asking, nothing in return
A wave, a smile!
A big hello!
till once again, the snow
shall fall—
He'll come back again,
I know!

Judy Bagley Welch

A Dream—A Vision

Behind closed eyes
I see a story-teller—
Whom I know well
some dark and oh so
gloomy, waiting to tell—
Just lying there
tied up inside—tight
not coming out—
Wrong way, not ready
You wait, wonder, true?
You ask—not sure
You ask—another story,
still lying there.
People! Sad, happy,
yearning, missing them!
Then up, you come,
with the almighty power,
through the blood-shot eyes of a buffalo—
Surprise at what has happened—the story you behold!
Amazement, laughter, smart remarks, all different,
as like some people we all know. Like maybe one we have
lost, lying in a casket—waiting until he bursts up with raging glory—
"For one day"—a true story he shall tell.
Unsure of what you have seen?
You question yourself—this can't be happening to me—
For I am that person lying in that casket.
Truth? Who I am—
for it's what's lying behind
closed eyes—
For the truth shall set me free!
Another story to be told.

Garland, Maine and the Old Maple Tree: Windows from My Soul

Fishing Tackle Basket—My Five Brothers

New at one time,
holding my many hooks, worms,
and fishing line—
maybe a book—
I carry you through the Alders of life,
listening for a babbling brook
I see in the distance
a sparkling little stream—
I set you down
opening you up
I wonder which hook shall
I use today?
Many years gone by
old and dirty
Your weave that once was
so tightly woven—now smells of
dried up
angle worms and apple cores shows its age.
But you will not be forgotten
Look! The fish I
brought home today!

Judy Bagley Welch

Attic of an Old Farm House

Many doors to wonder through
playing house, laughing, the smell
of old oats, stored up there
playing for hours in them!
really not aware
Until they all came pouring out!
"What are you kids doing?"
A voice came shouting out!
"Come down here!
Go outside and play"—
so down we would come
giggling all the way,
until the time for us to leave
"You must go home!"
Come play another day.

Neighbor Stranger

I do not know you as you not I!
We are new to each other,
we wonder why,
For we are like strangers,
'cause we have not yet met—
But we are our own neighbor
not soon to forget—
We may meet upon a path
or a busy walkway, only to
acknowledge to meet and greet someday.
For now you are my neighbor, no stranger, then am I—
for we are all now neighbors
in only passing by, we have met along the way—
to share a story, maybe how we met
that stranger, that first day.

Judy Bagley Welch

Riding on Angel Wings—A Dream

My oldest granddaughter
said to me last night,
"Nana, sweet dreams, good-night!"
And I did—
I awoke to riding on
Angel wings
An old branch has been broken
a little sad—you ask
But caught so soft and gentle—
Not a word or two
Was spoken—by a pair of
Angel wings
The colors oh so vivid—
feelings so divine
For another ring of life
has opened, in the
Big old tree of mine!

Garland, Maine and the Old Maple Tree: Windows from My Soul

Oliver Hill

Long dirt road ahead
Looking from the distance
Oh my! So far away
I'll climb you, someday
slipping, sliding, spinning—
ahead—back again
I keep going only to try
one more time
almost there, the top
is within my view,
the part, I know—so hard
back down again I go!

Hesitating, thinking, I will
go over you
Holding tight, another gear,
like gripping the wheel of life
I shall make it to the top
of this old dirt road
Looking back down from the top of Oliver Hill—

Judy Bagley Welch

Plowing of a Field

"Where do we start?"
So many rocks
smelling the freshly plowed
ground—I watch for
the next row to be unearthed.

Days are getting warmer
I taste the dust and sweat
I go on—
Not done yet
many more rows to plow my son—
Our work has only just begun
Rocks and sods!
"Where do they all come from?"
You have to ask?
We plow a field,
they have been here for many years,
my son
Tomorrow we shall pick them,
until there are no more. Again!
The dirt and dust will
greet us, resting on your skin,
only to return tomorrow
to do hard word again!

The Gift—My Writing, a Vision

My family just came to me
with their very own angel wings
They spoke to me—
Oh their voices of angels
how they ring
It has been so long they
have been gone, it seems
like eternity, they told
me not that long—
If only you believe
For they gave me praise
and glory, oh how their
faces glowed! The hugs,
the smiles, the tears, and laughter
of not so long ago—
I told them what I'm doing,
for they already knew
they have been waiting and watching
over me, helping me to believe, that's
the reason they came to me,
with their beautiful wings
from Heaven—the Gift!
If only you believe!

Judy Bagley Welch

The Old Plow Truck and I

I hear you shifting gears
coming up the hill
Blade down low
Snow upon your window
you slow down to take a peek—
only to see a light on,
on your way back down the road,
you stop
come inside—the coffee's hot!

Now it's snowing so much harder
than when I first set down
for the snowbanks will be
much higher covering the ground

Sliding will be better—for all the
young at heart
For I must be on my way
the snow is still falling
I plow another day

I see the sun it's peeking up
over in the East
Will there be school tomorrow?
I hope to get some sleep—
The banks are getting bigger—
radio is on—
Listening, just listening,
Canceled—

Garland, Maine and the Old Maple Tree: Windows from My Soul

Yes, it's dawn
I do not get much sleep, many more
roads to plow, yes, little ones
go back to sleep—no school now.
I shall lower my plow
and wing back the banks
that you may slide on today!
The rosy cheeks, frozen mittens;
I see them in my mind
soon not to be forgotten
Snow slows down as does
my plow and I, for we shall rest,
until again the snow shall fly—
we wait—the old plow truck and I!

Judy Bagley Welch

My Tiny Little Shealyn Rose—Heart Surgery

You came to us one morning
Seemed so perfect—not knowing
you were broken
Your mom and dad right there
to hold your tiny tender hands,
so soft and tender
for we knew in our hearts
and our minds you are a gift
from Heaven
God would mend the broken
branch in time—
Almost two years old now
God will hold your hand
and others one more time,
to mend the broken branch that's broken—
Mending us all in time.

Garland, Maine and the Old Maple Tree: Windows from My Soul

Tea Time

A tiny voice—I hear!
"Nana, let's have a tea party."
Shealyn, you sit right here.
Three of us now
talking and sipping.
Oh what a wonderful time!
It's such a beautiful day
for tea and crumpets,
how divine!

May I have some more? You reply,
"Why, sure!" Do you want more
tea and crumpets?
Shealyn, I'm asking you!

A smile, means yes!
That's what Shealyn is saying.
Her words aren't as proper
as yours and mine

For we eat our crumpets all up
and now we have no tea.
We'll wait until tomorrow.
Maybe another tea party
there may be.

Judy Bagley Welch

Mommy's Piggytails, Braids, Ponytails, and Ribbons

Mommy's piggytails, braids, ponytails, and ribbons,
These sit upon our heads
Two short, one long!
Hair too thin, piggy's gone.
Braids that have been
woven—oh what a beautiful sight
My braid is now a ponytail,
waving with delight.

Someday we'll want those
piggytails and braids and ponytails back.
Mommy, you do those just right—
you always pick just the right bow,
Sometimes you let us choose, sometimes no.

We will always remember the chair
you sit us in, to fix our hair
in piggytails, braids, ponytails and ribbons.

Daddy's Home—My Two Granddaughters and Daddy's Log Truck

We run to greet our daddy
the best in the whole world
We are the gifts from Heaven
Oh his precious little girls!

Daddy cooks us supper and
gets us ready for bed.
Maybe he will tell us a story
that's running through his head.

I hope it's one that Nana told him—
not that long ago, it does not matter
how the story's told, only to hear
our daddy tell it—
not so long ago.

"Tell it again Daddy!"
Our eyes are getting heavy
"Keep talking, for we still hear you."
"Sleep my little princesses!"
Daddy's hands and arms are still around you—
"As I kiss your tender cheeks,
sleep my little princesses,
Close your eyes, sweet dreams,
and sleep!"
Good-night.

Judy Bagley Welch

Maine Truckers—To My Son

Maine country woods truckers
stay at home mothers
from hauling logs to wood
chips and grain,
you old country woods truckers
up hills, taking spills, you young
and old gear jammers!

Don't care what kind of horses
are under your old hood,
You're just Maine country woods
truckers, hauling junk to cutting wood.

Many roads you men have traveled,
some stories you should not tell
but through your eyes, we see inside,
the devilish little grins as well—
Just Maine country woods truckers
hauling wood.

For my daddy was a Maine trucker
a damn good one, I might add
for he's no longer with me
though I'm a little sad
He taught me just as well
to grind the old gears and pop
that clutch, oh my God, it's Oliver Hill!

Move over you Maine country
wood truckers, for my Peter
wants to pass, Come on now, guys,
Just a little more—

Garland, Maine and the Old Maple Tree: Windows from My Soul

        Hey thanks, I guess!
        Now you can kiss my
   Maine country girls' ass-end!

     So now you know what
    my back door looks like—
   as well as my front, inside
      your old freightliner,
     and now "I" glance into
  my mirrors and see you back
      so far—oh my gosh!
        I read it wrong.
    You drive a Western Star?

   It's the thrill of the wheel beneath
  my hands, my foot is on the pedal.
   I pop the clutch, another gear
    up for this hill I must climb.
Overloaded with logs, driving through bogs
  for I'm a Maine country girl trucker.
The sound of my Jake, what a glorious sound,
    the smoke my stacks make,
for in my heart, I am a Maine country girl trucker.

    Maine trucking son of mine—
   for you too someday will have
  a Pete that you can call your own,
  to haul whatever you may choose,
  from hauling logs to hauling hogs
    wherever you may roam—

Judy Bagley Welch

Maybe down long highways
or trucking close to home,
still I know it's in your blood—
to pull that heavy load
from hauling wood and being good
wherever you may go.

Just wait my Maine country
woods trucker, one day it shall appear,
around a bend or corner
Your Peterbuilt will appear.

Shiny all chromed, from top to
bottom, color I hope you like
lights, oh so many lights!
With blue and red pin stripes!
Your name on both doors!
And on the back as well.

So now you have your own
New Peter-built
all shiny and brand new
To hauling the things you want to
From wood chips to logs
Watch out for swamps and bogs
You Maine country woods trucker,
That's you!

Pipe Organs

Bold, so loud
another Bud—I wait!
Hesitating—another ring
sounds, piercing through me
Still I wait
Strong, but also
gentle, sometimes
Ringing, oh so loud!
Stinging, like an angry
yellow jacket, through your skin,
You also feel the sting
Dark and gloomy
I'm listening, waiting,
Do I hear the voice
of pipe organs, pushing
echoing, adrenaline running
through me?
I wait, listening like
the sap that also runs through
my limbs
But
Today I hear pipe organs
only soft and gentle ones
Missing—
If only to go back for a moment
to hear those pipe organs ring

Judy Bagley Welch

The Old Pot

Peeking through another window
looking I see,
the old pot
sometimes full, sometimes not
Gathering the food to place
in it, dropping some on the ground—
Family and friends
just stopping in
I gathered more to place
I hesitate in question!
Do I place all what I
have gathered, dropping
some upon the ground?
For my pot if still
half-empty—Still I find
enough to go around.
Today my pot was emptied,
Now waiting again to be filled
not knowing what and where
I'll go to gather to put in
or—how full it may be
I may place a tator,
that has grown underground,
an onion, a carrot or string-bean
My pot again is filling up, it appears
to be quite full, I hesitate
I know there is something missing—I remember now
it's the peas! So I will try to remember to fill and empty
at the end of each day, so the old pot will always be empty
So in the morning in case
family and friends come
I will always be ready
To fill that old pot again!

I'll Wait

I'll wait silently—still
sun is coming up over
from the East, to help me grow
another day is born.
That I may grow another
limb for you to set upon
the warmth and light
that shines through me
shall shine also across the road.
Curtains opening up
Oh what a wonderful sight
to be sitting on
Oliver Hill
I'm waiting
I grow—not knowing, waiting
for the pane/pain—
"None broken"
Not today, I see
For all the curtains are open
the sun is shining through
I sit and grow deep roots
On Oliver Hill, a small town
called Garland, Maine.

Judy Bagley Welch

Past and Future

Yesterday, knocked from my tree!
to lie beside my tree,
I lie helpless on the ground
I say, "Oh no, not me!"
It has taken many years
to climb to be where I should be,
for you mustn't knock me to the ground
to lie beneath my tree—
For I will climb back
to where I once was
grasping limb by limb
For I choose not to be
Knocked off
To hit the ground again!

Family, Friend, and Feast

You called—I answered
You asked, we thought
For what shall we
all eat?
We gathered, placing it on
your table
Our eyes opened wide
Oh, what a wonderful feast!
We then sat there
just talking
Laughing 'bout old times
Looking at photos—snapshots
passing through our eyes
For now our bellies are so full,
darkness all around, we must be going,
only to return again to feast
upon your table another day
My family and our friend.
For it's not that far
just a short trot
to another small Maine town—
called Ripley, believe it or not!

Judy Bagley Welch

Today I Received My Class One—My Son Teaching Me on the Golden Road with My Permit

Today I received my class one,
I've dreamt of for so long
I know not what I'll
drive—a Pete or a Mack
All I see is you right there.
Proud—oh so proud
Sitting beside me,
Smiling we are smiling
grins from ear to ear
One gear up, two gears down
the road appears to narrow,
So don't worry Mom,
There's another trip tomorrow
Although mine seems
so different from the one
you now hold—
No—not really—
As down the "Golden Road" of
Life we go
You teach me
I'll listen
As I taught you, my son
For today—I realized
through my words, written
and spoken—I received my class one!

The Watering Hole Gathering

I stopped just for a while
Entering, I sat down
I see the smiling faces
I asked, you gave
In the distance I hear
laughter, lights down dim
we all are friends
if only it's our first meeting
We may talk about old history
long ago, maybe an old horse that
once walked to this town
carrying a piece of iron to
place upon the ground
I hear not far away
An old man's voice
"Hey, he just threw a shoe,"
He's going to be okay.

For today "I gathered," not knowing
the towns in which I've lived,
all one time were just one parcel—
from Stetson, Maine
Oh not I
to another small town, another
small dot called Ripley, Maine,
Believe it or not!
For now I reside in Dexter, Maine.
But roots will live on, I will go back
someday, to my small home town where my heart will always be—
To sit upon Oliver Hill Garland, Maine, like the roots under my old
Maple Tree.

Judy Bagley Welch

Whispers, Giggles, Grins

I was awoken today to see the face
of a wise old man, who lived just
down the road a piece.
I put my arms around you
I smile
Whispers, giggles, grins
For today I sat at your table
looking across I see
Dripping from your chin from
the chew you just put in
For you are quite the prankster
Untold secrets you withhold as
well as I—
For today I shall to you one
not that long ago
A tear may drop upon my table
like the drop from upon your chin—
Oh where do I start? I smile
Whispers, giggles, grins!
Now our families go far back
from upon the old hill, to just down
around the corner—a story I shall tell!
Although—I'm sure you already knew
that my oldest, middle, youngest
is your first and oldest grandson
that was raised upon the hill,
also is a part of you.
People shall talk for my secret
is now out, my heart's oh so much lighter,
proudness within—for your second son was my first love,
for love is not a sin, now I sit at my table, no more whispers,
only giggles and happy grins.

Swing

How shall we make it?
An old grain bag stuffed with
hay or straw, tied together
by a piece of bailing twine
Beams—too high!
The ladder we must climb
throw the rope over—
let it fall, we shall swing
on a bag of hay and straw
tied together with another
piece of bailing twine
Hey wait, we'll all
climb on together
Swinging to and fro
Hold on tight for all
your might—bailing twine's
a breaking!
Laughs so loud
Down we go
Landing in the musty hay and straw
Hey that wasn't that scary,
Now let's walk the beams—
not much higher from the
rope we just threw over, you go first
we will follow—eyes oh so big
and so much higher—come on, we'll all
hold hands! Is everyone ready? You really
have to ask. Now only one step at a time—
Hey, look at us! We are walking across the old beam
just like that old grain bag swing, made from musty hay and straw,
held together by a piece of bailing twine.

Judy Bagley Welch

Boards, Knot, One Hole

You took an old board—cutting holes
not quite the right size
we carried that board with us—
Not knowing, or could see
holes that you had cut out
wrong, so wrong!
Though many treasures we've brought home,
thinking it was right
Smiling—carrying them
in an old stocking, holding
them so tight, gathering
through that old board that you had made
Through my eyes now
I see another board
That gave us so much pleasure
Rolling—just rolling
Knot's gone—hole's there—
this board is so much better
In my heart those memories
I will always treasure.

Thoughts, Dreams, Visions

Thinking fast
Eyes seeing
Beautiful—all around!
The hill where I once lived
and was wed!
I was there—
thoughts, dreams, visions
Children
playing, laughing, swinging,
friends sipping tea
and coffee
chatting 'bout old times—
Pictures
old—new
Oh look!
I remember that one!
What a glorious time
Everyone I hear is welcome
no matter the season
don't need a reason, or a
special day—
Bring friends, families
set upon the hill
Reading old stories, photos, and snapshots,
you may have known or heard of
Paths
across the field

Judy Bagley Welch

Little feet running across them
or swings to swing upon,
"parents"

Sitting upon the ground
picnic's all around!
Worries?
None!
Maybe someday—maybe!
This scene will become
true again—
If only in my
thoughts, dreams, visions
I
Give these memories to you!

Garland, Maine and the Old Maple Tree: Windows from My Soul

Pig Skin

One picture, I hold in my mind
I will always treasure
maybe you recall as well—
Five (brothers) played
but three played at one
time together—
Although, not from your town
just a little east
you know the name
they gave their all
think!
You may recall
Not only for their town
but your town as well
Those three that played together
came from upon the hill!
Not sitting on the bench,
they went to the front line
Knowing exactly what that meant,
Not holding nothing back
giving all they had!
Sweat, blood, sometimes tears,
they pushed through,
Oh that wasn't so bad.
Many years, the name showed up,
to stand on that white line
Still not carrying—though they didn't mind,
they knew their job was to protect and guard that old white line—
Now maybe you can go back in time, and maybe you will see
the same one that I have been seeing—
Five brothers played
throughout the years
But three all played at
one time together!

Judy Bagley Welch

Five Line-Men

Five linemen—also from my home town
among so many others
"metal" beneath their feet
to stand upon that line,
just like many moons that have gone by, just like bringing
"that piece of iron" to the town
where you may reside
Smiling faces, clapping hands,
Listen, do you hear?
Cheers from all the people
Running, walking, standing oh so still,
Hands upon their chests
only for a moment
paying respect like they had
been taught—
Waiting, hearts pounding, blood
running through their veins,
Intense! Ready?
Hands behind that line!
All five stood at one time
or another—three oldest
stood together, one time behind
that line
I can recall two youngest also,
played just as well together—

Those very special five linemen
whom I know so very well, also lived
on Oliver Hill—a small town called Garland, Maine.
So now I'm sure a few folks can recall
the name I have not written
though hoping you will remember—
Maybe someday to pass a memory on from you!
Whom you may also hold, maybe in your arms
to tell about this story of five linemen
who stood behind that line.

My Son—Three Times You Came

Upon waking
Full moon, I see. Fee,.
Cold wind blowing
a small flame, or maybe
a flicker
No!
Keep going
waiting—oh so patiently—
morning shall come—
peeking through my window
just cresting atop of the trees
Oh my
Look peeking back at me
The sun/my son has come—bringing
warmth again today
Thanking him upon his leaving,
for again He shall return.
Only a little flicker
Flame is going out
not worried. I won't be
cold again tonight.
Again!
Working, thinking!
Not giving up
Both sets of hands—so cold!
Gathering we went inside
Watching, waiting, for the flame
to give more heat
Yes! It's going
not giving up—no defeat!
We smile,

Judy Bagley Welch

You ride away,
see. One more time
today.
"You!"
For my flame, for sure this
time has gone out
So cold, you gather
Alone this time
Gathering from a friend,
pieces to bring back, just
like the questions you may
have asked—
Yes!
You—we did it for the flame
is so bright and oh so much warmer—
I asked three times
"You came!"
To bring warmth not only just for you,
But for me,
Your mother.

Garland, Maine and the Old Maple Tree: Windows from My Soul

Yesterday

Spoke with my sister
We talked and laughed
Things we were doing today
and also some things we talked
about in the past
I'm going to watch
my two granddaughters
not sure what we'll play
two runny little noseys
not so pink cheeks
do I see
"Nana, will you hold us?"
Come on, climb up,
For I shall read you two
a book, sit still, and learn
and listen, you may hear—
"Hey, it's Daddy, we can
help him cook!"
The smiles are back as well as
pink cheeks—noseys still dripping
Now sit up and eat your supper!
"Nana, will you stay a little longer?
Until we fall asleep?"
Daddy asks,
"What did you girls do today?"
"We picked up our rooms to help you and Mommy,
then Nana said, 'Now let's play.'"
Okay, it's getting late—
Daddy can we lay on yours and Mommy's bed?

Judy Bagley Welch

Come on Nana!
Okay, lie still—
Nana, sing us a song.
Red River Valley?
No, not that one!
Eyes are getting heavy
arms around you both tight
sandman is coming to bring
sweet dreams tonight—
Glancing, as I stand
to leave, not only are their
eyes closed, I look also at my son,
who is also sleeping peacefully
Bending down, I kiss
three faces, walking quietly
out the door.
Sweet dreams, good-night,
Sweet dreams.
I'll be back again tomorrow!

One Name—Upon an Envelope

Maybe an old tooth brush
or a pair of child's blunt shears
No!
not yet!
Don't open, touch or use
one lesson you all will learn today
to pass on to one another
The word "inside" you will
not see, only the name!
Upon the envelope that
taught us many lessons
taught at home first, passing
down many generations—
maybe—bumps or bruises
Frowns or tears, it only
made us stronger, through
humiliation or fear!
Now you may recall
the name—written upon the envelope
for I learned the word
inside
I passed onto my one child
"a word is not just a word,"
It's how and to whom it is
spoken!
So now you should know the
word, yes! It is
"Respect"
Remember that one word when speaking
to whomever that may be—that word will be a lesson,
not only for you who does it, but surely it
will stay with me!

Judy Bagley Welch

Snow Angels and Snow Bunnies

Snow had fallen the
night before
warm breeze blowing
sunshine all around
"Hey, Mommy and Nana!
Can we go make snow angels?"
All bundled up
like snow bunnies
we headed outdoors
Our little faces all aglow
Mommy digging tunnels
We and Nana on the sled
high upon the bank—
"Ready?"
Hang on!
Here we go!
Eyes so big and mouth opened wide
Down the bank we go
Sliding, slipping across the yard—
Now can we make
Snow angels?
Mommy and Nana all at one time
picked us up, and plopped us in the snow—
Wave your arms and legs!
Then picked us up by the front
of our suits, all in just one motion
Us two little sisters
didn't even have a notion
"Hey, look!
There are your snow angels!

Garland, Maine and the Old Maple Tree: Windows from My Soul

Mommy, Nana,
they look like snow bunnies!"
We smile
Don't worry, snow angels
or snow bunnies,
two new stars will
shine tonight—
"Mommy, Nana, come look
in our bed—
A big star fell from Heaven—
Oh thank you!"
You told us to just believe,
landing on our pillow
Great big smiles
Glistening eyes
for tonight—there are
two new stars
Snow angels or snow bunnies
It doesn't really matter
Snow angels or snow bunnies
We told you they would let
you know in some special
little way, once they made it
way up high
If you really look,
You two can see your two.
Because all the stars up in the sky
are snow angels or snow bunnies
Twinkling back at you!

Judy Bagley Welch

Old Rags, Old Rug, New Yarn, New Flag

Hundred year old hands, that I have held, as they also held mine
    Love and care that ran through them,
  also through things they have made.

      Knowledge, wisdom,
      caring, greatest of all,
          Love!
      Tear it just right!
      Tie it in a knot!
  Now tie them all together!
  Wooden hook—up then down
      under, around
    Pull—look you did it!
        I smile
  It shall be as nice as the
    one you made for me!
  Be sure and lie it flat
So it doesn't curl when people
      Step on it—
      Excuse me,
this will never touch the ground—
    not the rug that you
      made for me.

Garland, Maine and the Old Maple Tree: Windows from My Soul

It's just as important
like the chocolate ice cream
that you so dearly loved—
or the angels you had collected
throughout your beings here—
You taught me how to make
an old rug from rags, for "my hands"
have made something new
Except I made the
Dear old flag
for my son—also
to never touch the ground!

So, you see, my 100-year-olds!
I have learned and taught as well
to my son,
to respect and love thy neighbor
like all the flags that have flown,
not just our red, white, and blue,
but like so many others and colors
not to touch the ground,
Oh so true!
Some day soon well all
become one!

Judy Bagley Welch

"Nana, What Does God Look Like?"

My two granddaughters and I were
swinging out back
beautiful day, sun shining.
My oldest granddaughter asked,
"Nana, what does God look like?"
I told her—do you see the
trees, grass, flowers, sky?
You and sister, Mommy, Daddy,
everyone you love?
That's what God looks like.
Oh yes, and also butterflies!
She then said, "Nana,
I see God's face!"
You do?
What does it look like to you?
"Round!"
I smiled and told her
that's exactly right—
we are all one!
We are every living thing
in that round circle that
God has created for all of
us to see—called life!

Christmas Tea

I heard there's going to be a
Christmas party tea
I'm sure you know who told me,
'cause he came to your home last night
With all his magic reindeer
on his once a year big flight!

He told me it was going to be at your Nana's,
and he didn't mind who came
I hope you don't mind but he invited also
two new friends who have not
yet no names!

Some old friends also stopped
in to join you, Garfield, Four-winds,
baby Dolly, Bunny, Mylina, Nana,
and me—Annie.

So from now on, we can always
get together on Christmas Eve,
then wait till Christmas morning
to have our Christmas tea,
with your new friends and dollies
whomever they may be.

Judy Bagley Welch

Apron Strings and Wings
To my loving son, Heath Bagley

I remember your first little flutter
inside me, letting me know
you wanted to be free—
and you rolled and tumbled inside my tummy,
and I knew that moment, you wanted me as your mommy
I nurtured and loved you, the way I was shown, knowing
that someday you would be all grown.
You and I would laugh, sing, and play
and in the back of my mind,
I would dread the "big day."

Well, it's here my only son,
It's time to cut those
apron strings
Fly high my child
Here are your wings!

Do not be afraid, this is just
part of your life
You're married now, you took a wife
Be proud, be happy and someday you too
will make Mom and Dad, Grammy and Grampy.

Take these wings, keep them
close to your heart,
and remember we will always
love you, together or apart!
Although son, we may be apart,
take out your
wings and hold them close
to your heart!

Garland, Maine and the Old Maple Tree: Windows from My Soul

All mom and dad's love
is inside them
they will keep you safe and secure
So—spread your wings, son
and you will soar!

Do not be afraid, son,
Mom's untied the strings!
Soar high, my little son,
and spread your wings.

These wings were your Nanny's
and now they are mine
I give them to you, son,
in hopes you will fly.
Spread your wings, son, no matter
what the future brings,
for that big day will come
when you, too, cut those strings!

It's a real hard thing to do,
but we all must abide
and let our wings unfold
and enjoy the ride.
Life is full of ups and downs.

That's why God gave us all wings
to keep us from getting down—
So son, when you are
feeling down and alone,
Just close your eyes
and hold these little wings
and you will feel home!

Judy Bagley Welch

Team of Great White Horses
In memory of my youngest brother Larry

You drove a team of ponies
You played an old guitar
You sang the songs our momma wrote,
You wished upon a star!

You drove a team of horses
You played a new guitar
You sang the songs our momma wrote
You wished upon a star!

You took blue ribbons, red, gold and white
You played your old guitar
On your wagon under a full moon
So bright!

You drove a team of horses
Called—Lady and Gene
You played an old guitar
And sang songs that our
Momma sang.

But now you drive a team of great white horses
And play a silver guitar—
You took the songs our momma wrote
And sing them above the stars!

You might have never went to Nashville
or the Grand Ole Opry,
But you sing up in the heavens
On the one and only big screen TV!

You now sing with Williams,
Frezel, Husky, and Cline,
Twitty, Reeves, and Solvine!

So you see, you really did make it big
With your ponies and guitar and songs
You drive that eight hitch team of great white horses
And sing the songs our momma sang at home.

Garland, Maine and the Old Maple Tree: Windows from My Soul

Last Night, Beside My Bed I Knelt

I knelt last night beside my bed,
I've not done that in years
I clasped my hands together
and I prayed between each tear,
I prayed old Lord, give me strength
to get through these troubled times,
to make my family whole again,
through the tears I felt divine!

I didn't really ask for much
like money, wealth or fame
I asked for stuff like
give love and faith to the
little children, the needy, and
the rich, the old, the young,
and troublesome, and of course,
the very sick—

You see Lord! my youngest brother
became very ill—You came one day
and made him well
I watched him suffer through his pain—
knowing down the road
he'd have everything to gain
And you came dear Lord
one precious morn—you took him home,
no more, I mourn—
for now I know he'll be
home tomorrow, no more pain,
no more sorrow—
I pray each night
for proper things, through
the tears of prayer, I hear
him sing, that's what will
make my family whole again!

Judy Bagley Welch

The Great Tree Stand
My son's first bear hunt

I head down the road with my
gun in hand
headed for the perfect tree stand
I drag behind me, donuts and grain,
just to find out I have
half of a tree stand.

I stand there in awe!
What shall I do now?
I really hope that big bear
is not on the prowl
my four buddies
have left me to find
their own spot, hope when
they get there—
they have what I've not!

This is my first bear hunt
hope I don't mess my pants
if the big one gives a big grunt.

One guy will come back—
and check on us on rounds,
hopefully he doesn't see me
sitting on the ground
guess I'll try and fix
my stand, then I will at least
be off the ground
I sat patiently in my seat—
Holy-shit! He's smelling my seat!
I do not move for
I am in shock—
Do I drop my gun
or grab my crotch?
I'm breathing really fast,
my heart is so pounding!

Garland, Maine and the Old Maple Tree: Windows from My Soul

I turn to the right
and realize I shoot
left handed—
God let this great tree stand
hold up and not leave
me grounded—

I look through my sights,
what do I see? A little
bear cub who's messing with me.
I know momma's close at hand,
Damn, don't I wish I had
a bigger tree stand?

I did not get one on my
first outing, I'm back here today,
hopefully, we will all do some shooting.

It does not really matter what I see today.
One thing I know, it's not getting away—
small, medium, or large, it's not going to matter,
it's going home with me no matter
how my teeth chatter.
I hear a noise below on my ladder.
I look down to see, it's a little chipmunk
taking a pee! I think to myself,
God I wish he would leave!
I'm not really sure
how much more weight
should be on my ladder,
My kidneys are full
so I empty my bladder!

It's getting dark now
we head out of the woods
God let them come
back to where this great
tree stand stood!

Judy Bagley Welch

Silently I Wait—Me Waiting for My Son to Come Out of the Woods

"Shhh," I hear a branch snap,
I listen with the ears of a deer
I wait, nothing!
Silently I wait
I look around me in awe—
and I see nothing!
And again, I hear and listen.
I hear the wind whistle
through the trees!
"Shhh," I hear a twig break!
I hear with the ears of a deer
and I see with the eyes of an owl.
Nothing, silently I wait!
Dusk will come soon, silently I wait
I can smell evening approaching
I wait silently
"Shhh," I'm as still as a fox, my senses
also as sharp
I wait!
Nothing!
Silently I wait
"Shhh" I hear birds in the distance
Nothing—again!
Silently I wait
My senses alive with curiosity
You ask why I wait?
I wait for the great hunt!
Silently I wait
I look and I see, I listen and I hear,
I smell and I taste
I touch and I feel
Silently I wait

Garland, Maine and the Old Maple Tree: Windows from My Soul

Evening dew is upon the trees
I feel it and taste it also
upon my face
Silently I wait
Again you ask why I wait?
The great hunt, I reply.

One who has walked this
great Earth for many years,
one who is wise, one who
we can learn from,
"Shhh," I hear again!
Nothing!
Silently I wait
I am not alone for he is out
there waiting also!
Silently
Why? you ask again.
I reply,
The great bear!

www.ingramcontent.com/pod-product-compliance
Lightning Source LLC
Chambersburg PA
CBHW031202090426
42736CB00009B/763